CCXP EXAM PREPARATION

Michael G. Bartlett, PMP, CCXP

First Edition: March 2017

Revised Edition: January 2018

A MeasureOfTruth.co product

Sketches kindly donated by Steve Simmons www.airworksart.com

CONTENTS

A WORD FROM THE AUTHOR

The **Certified Customer Experience Professional** (CCXP) is one of the toughest exams I have ever taken. Unlike other professional exams, which can be passed by simply memorizing a body of knowledge and applying common sense, the CCXP is an exam that can confuse even seasoned professionals and force you to draw on nuanced real world experience to deduce the correct answers.

That being said, I have spoken with many accomplished Customer Experience professionals in the field who have actually failed the exam; I, myself, failed on my first attempt. Many times you will find yourself thinking "it depends" when you narrow a question down to one of two answers. Missteps on these crucial questions can be the difference between passing and failing.

This book contains a set of principles that really helped me with the exam. When preparing to sit for the exam a second time, I started organizing all of my material into a framework that I could easily recall and use to guide me. The pages that follow contain this information.

I will stress that this book should be used as *supplementary* material. For primary training, I recommend two CXPA Authorized Resource & Training Providers. Lynn Hunsaker of *ClearAction* and Ian Golding of *Customer Experience Consultancy Ltd.* I used both as my primary study sources when preparing for the exam and can personally vouch for their effectiveness. I also strongly recommend you use my CCXP Exam Simulator to make sure you are truly CCXP ready.

Throughout this book, I have bolded a lot of key terms. I strongly recommend that you research these further as part of your exam prep.

Michael Bartlett, PMP, CCXP

Branson, MO, March 2017

PROFITS FROM THIS BOOK

All of us have passions outside of the good work we do in a professional capacity. My biggest passion is helping animals.

It all began for me on a summer evening in July 2015, when my wife and I rescued a beagle who had been dumped on the side of a rural Missouri road. He had five broken ribs, and was covered in fleas and ticks. We took him to the emergency clinic in Springfield, Missouri, not sure if he would live. After spending eight weeks with us in recovery, we fell in love with him and adopted him. I named him Basil.

Shortly after this, I started volunteering with Tri-Lakes Humane Society in Reeds Spring, Missouri and other no-kill shelters and foster networks.

Every penny of profit due to me will be sent to an animal charity that has been personally vetted by myself.

Since its launch in March 2017, the book has helped many students with their exam prep and donated over $2,000 to numerous animal shelters and charities.

If you purchased a copy from Amazon, please drop me a line at **Mike@MeasureOfTruth.co** and I will let you know which animals directly benefited from your purchase.

FOREWORD BY LORI KIRKLAND

When I waited tables, a wise guest once said *"You are only as good as your last happy customer."*

I think this advice is true for organizations as well. In a world where we all have raised expectations of customer interactions, it is more critical than ever to understand and focus on improving those experiences from a human perspective. Understanding the field and practice of Customer Experience (CX) requires a shift in thinking and a focus on the humans involved.

Michael has done a fantastic job of highlighting the key foundations of CX best practices and clearly outlined how to quickly start implementing these practices. His overview of core principles and the reasoning behind them will help you to pass the Certified Customer Experience Professional exam.

If you are new to CX, this book is a great guidepost to help you start thinking about the core tenants of the industry and introduce ideation to make you successful.

The CX community needs more resources like this.

Enjoy & Good luck on the exam.

Lori Kirkland, CCXP

Chief Experience Officer

Terrapin Digital

SECTION 1

KEY PRINCIPLES

PRINCIPLE 1:
FRAME MARKETS BY JOBS-TO-BE-DONE

One of the biggest revelations in the world of CX is that markets should be defined by the needs of customers, not by product or industry. These needs were termed "Jobs to be done" (JTBD) by influential author, *Clayton Christensen*. Christensen argued that unless you truly understand the needs of the users of your product, you can never truly innovate. Focusing on the functional aspects of a product, alone, is not enough.

By bringing a human-centered lens, as opposed to an industry lens, to look at customers, it is possible to see them in new and original ways.

A single JTBD is specific to discrete customer types and occasions and is typically written as an actionable statement, such as: *buy a car*. But it could also be *to look successful*. Or *to feel safe*. JTBD can be either emotional or functional in nature. These combine to create an overall purchasing behavior which can then be molded into what we in the CX world call a **Persona**.

In addition to understanding the JTBD, you should also understand the key drivers behind them. Below is an example showing elements of a particular Persona's JTBD and example drivers:

JTBD when buying a car	Example Driver
Feel Safe	Has newborn baby
Look to project success	Hoping for promotion
Cost under $20,000	Single Family income; tight budget
Avoid painful and expensive repairs	Single Family income; tight budget
Large Trunk	Family Shopping

These drivers will help to further refine your understanding of your customers.

PRINCIPLE 2:
PERSONAS SHOULD EMPHASISE EXPECTATIONS

A number of different elements can make up a persona. We have already reviewed Jobs-To-Be-Done and Job Drivers.

Personas should also contain information about the environment that the persona exists in and any pain points that they may experience. Together all of this information informs us about what matters most and is valued by a Persona.

This information will lead to the creation of expectations. There are two types: Implicit and Explicit expectations.

When a persona interacts with your business, their expectations will be based on the information above (Jobs, Drivers, Circumstances, etc.), and the expectation of the Customer Experience that your business, whether explicitly or implicitly, sets.

If you dine out for the evening at a fine restaurant, you would not expect to wait an hour before someone takes your order. That is an example of an implicit expectation. These are set through various means: cultural norms, industry norms, word of mouth, common decency, and so forth.

If you went to buy a car and the slogan was *"No hassle buying"*, you would not expect to be accosted by a slimy salesman as soon as you set foot on the lot. That is an example of an explicit expectation, set clearly by marketing.

Expectations are important as they can help inform what **Value** means to a persona, which, in turn, can help you ensure your **Value Proposition** is framed correctly.

PRINCIPLE 3:
PERCEIVED VALUE = EXPERIENCE ÷ EXPECTATIONS

Value is the take-away of an experience. If you've ever heard someone say a product or experience was "not good value for money" it is because they expected more based on what they paid. CX Management is as much about managing expectations as it is managing the sum of the experience, not just how much it costs, with the intention of creating value for the customer.

Businesses need to think carefully about how they frame their **Value Proposition**. This is done through a combination of their **Brand Attributes** and how they market and execute their **Branded Customer Experience**. That is, an experience that is *designed* to meet the specific needs of a specific target group.

Part of the consideration should be setting expectations for what parts of the experience, or which experiences, will be delightful and which will be mediocre or on par with competitors. You can't be the best at everything.

One thing to always remember: improving the Customer Experience adds Value. The greater value that customers perceive, the greater amounts they will pay for your product or service.

PRINCIPLE 4:
STAGES BEFORE TOUCHPOINTS

Once you have your personas, you know who your customers are. Now you need to know what they do to achieve their goals and satisfy their JTBD. You need to start thinking about their individual customer journeys. For each **Customer Journey**, it is a good idea to map out the broad stages of the experience before delving into the **touchpoints** (moments when the customer interacts with the business) and potentially getting lost in the weeds.

In some cases, there may be too many touchpoints to realistically map out while maintaining a 10,000 ft. view of the customer journey. The key is to always maintain a holistic view of the journey from the customer's perspective.

Start with the broad phases of the journey. Use whatever data you have available to you and consider involving customers in the exercise. It is paramount that your business fully appreciates and understand the end-to-end customer journey before you begin getting into the details.

PRINCIPLE 6:
FRONT-LINE EMPLOYEES HAVE VALUABLE INSIGHTS

Front Line Employees will typically have already amassed a lot of insight into the **Voice of the Customer**. They will be able to help provide information about some of the touchpoints and which ones they feel have the biggest **pain points** associated with them.

Typically touchpoints with large pain points will be clear candidates for CX improvement initiatives.

Another term you will likely hear is "**Moment of Truth**." The term was first introduced by Richard Normann and popularized by Jan Carlzon in his 1987 book of that name. He used the term to mean those moments in which there is an opportunity for an organization to make a difference when interacting with a customer.

By drilling into the **Voice of the Employee** – that is, insights about the customer experience gathered from employees - it is possible to see which touchpoints are the biggest drivers of satisfaction and loyalty. It follows that these should also be the most important to the business. Therefore, this is why these are typically referred to as the moment of truth.

PRINCIPLE 7:
RELIABILITY MATTERS MORE THAN WOW MOMENTS

A Customer Experience is only as good as its weakest link.

According to a recent study by the London School of Economics, there is a 300% revenue gain to be had if reliability is prioritized over 'wow' moments. This is because negative word-of-mouth is more powerful than positive word-of-mouth, in terms of influencing customer behavior.

Imagine a five-star restaurant that you frequent, where the price is right, the service is wonderful, the food is immaculate and the ease of reserving a table is effortless. And then imagine there was a one off experience with a hair in your food. Or a one off experience with a rude waiter.

Imagine a telephone banking experience where you provide basic credentials and get great service, year-in, year-out. Whenever you call, you know exactly what to expect. And then the experience suddenly changes as a result of security process changes; suddenly you asked for information you don't have or are unsure about; then they unceremoniously hang up on you! Now you are unable to get your banking done without a lot of frustration and a visit to the local branch to find out what is going on.

Experiences should be reliably *consistent*. If an experience is inconsistent, it can damage your brand. 95% of customers tell others about a bad experience. If your experience has to change, for whatever reason, it needs to be effectively communicated to reset expectations.

PRINCIPLE 8:
AN OUNCE OF PREVENTION IS WORTH A POUND OF CURE

Benjamin Franklin's famous quote about fire-safety applies just as appropriately to Customer Experience.

Most Customer Experience efforts begin with trying to understand the customer and their goals. They then move to sustained efforts to eliminate pain points and improve journeys.

True CX transformation happens when the organization is able to focus on preventing issue occurrence or re-occurrence.

In terms of services, this means **Doing It Right The First Time**. Tools and quality approaches such as *Lean* and *Six Sigma* can help with process mapping and improvement, helping to reduce waste and rework.

There is also a great benefit to be had from reducing the time spent firefighting by employees. The less time they spend doing that, the more time they have to participate in value-added activities.

PRINCIPLE 9:
IT'S ALL ABOUT THE BENJAMINS

There he is, again. Benjamin Franklin now features in two principles, consecutively!

Except, this time we're talking money.

One thing you should never forget is that Customer Experience always leads back to the bank balance. The reason businesses exist is because of their customers. This is why *Jeanne Bliss*, the author of *Chief Customer Officer 2.0*, says we should treat customers as Assets.

It should always be remembered that cash is the lifeblood of a business, and without customers, there is no cash.

This means that when a CX professional wants to persuade their CEO to fund a CX program, they must be able to show that in the long run the CX program will be healthy for the balance sheets.

One key way of doing this is to tie CX metrics to existing Business Metrics, so there is a clear case that improving Customer Satisfaction leads to improved revenue.

PRINCIPLE 10:
ALIGN THE SILOS

Implementing a CX Strategy from the ground up can be likened to a political campaign. It is a good idea to meet one-on-one with other leaders across the organization as part of a culture assessment to assess where the land lies. Without a strong network of ambassadors, it will be impossible to operationalize the program.

One way to build support is to frame the problem as a shared one. The teams will understand that each plays a vital role and that they will need to engage together.

The ultimate goal of all this political maneuvering is to get to a point where reporting, measurements and terminology can be aligned across silos so the effort becomes a true one-company campaign, resulting in a genuine culture shift.

Without taking the time to make these first steps, there is a risk of launching 10,000 ships in different, albeit well meaning, directions.

PRINCIPLE 11:
CULTURE IS NURTURED, NOT MANDATED

Culture is what we do when the boss in not in the office! It's our default way of thinking and doing without any governance.

No amount of financial incentives or threats can make an employee care about a customer. In-fact, it can be argued that ambitious bonus targets will encourage corners to be cut and rushed delivery – thus nurturing an anti-customer centric culture!!

The best ways to build a true Customer Centric organization are to:

- Hire employees who have a natural affinity for customer centricity.
- Create the appropriate environment so that new and existing employees are set up to deliver great experiences. You can't expect employees to deliver great experiences if you are forever throwing hurdles, such as bad processes or lack of training, in their way. Compensation should only be tied to Customer Centric metrics once this environment is in place.
- Share customer stories across the organization, not just in the odd silo or two. This will help employees build empathy as stories work better than charts. A **Customer Room** can also help employees to step into the world of the customer.
- Create an Operational Code of Conduct to guide behaviors and decisions.
- Management must lead by example.

As *Kerry Bodine* points out in her book, *Outside In*, *"Companies that jump straight to instituting formal rewards risk having employees focus on doing the bare minimum to get their payouts instead of working to develop customer-centric behavior."*

PRINCIPLE 12:
CULTURE + GOVERNANCE = EXECUTION

A strong customer centric culture should be combined with strong governance practices to help drive execution and excellence.

Examples of good governance practices include:

- Closing the loop with customers who provided feedback. This will help build confidence that you take their input seriously and are willing to act.
- Not asking a question on a survey without ensuring that question has an owner who will be responsible for taking action based on answers.
- Keeping a list or a top ten of Customer Experience Improvement opportunities for future projects, including which senior executive is accountable for resolution.
- Holding individuals accountable for touchpoints so that issues do not slip through the cracks or end up with Silos passing the buck.
- Add Customer Experience criteria to all new project proposals.
- Introduce and then reinforce CX Standards. This should be an ongoing effort, in person, with face-to-face debate; a PowerPoint presentation e-mailed out will not stick.
- Keep the standards simple so they become ingrained.

PRINCIPLE 13:
BIG DATA DOES NOT TELL YOU 'WHY'

Quantitative data is useful for providing information such as which web pages on a site were visited most frequently, and the length of time spent on each page. They can help you track purchasing patterns and trends. They can help you track peak times for call center volume. But they can't tell you the motivation behind them. Why did someone call the helpdesk? Why did they click through to checkout but never actually complete their transaction?

This is where open-ended questions in surveys and qualitative research comes in.

Qualitative research includes:

- Phone transcripts
- Chat/e-mail transcripts
- Customer Diaries
- One-on-one Interviews with Customers
- Observations
- Voice of Employee programs (See Principle 6)

A regular survey won't be able to tell you this information unless you knew the answers in advance and were able to structure the survey appropriately. This just does not happen in the real world.

PRINCIPLE 14:
ACTIONS SPEAK LOUDER THAN WORDS

In terms of being able to predict business results based on customer data, actions always speak louder than words. It is very hard for a customer to tell you what they would do in an unfamiliar situation.

Customer behaviors are much more reliable.

The other benefit to actual actions taken is that they can be linked to operational data since both occur in a specific time and place.

In 2013, Kohl's were able to take advantage of the reliability of actions over words by testing out new store hours on a small subset of their locations. Had they surveyed shoppers, the results would not have been as reliable. But by looking at actual behavioral results in their test group, they were able to move ahead with confidence that the new hours would not affect sales.

In terms of instilling confidence in employees and customers, actual actions aimed at improving the customer experience, backed up by the sharing of these wins, obviously go a lot further than lip service.

Furthermore, when looking at CX training and communications within an organization, the old adage applies again. Training should be hands on and relatable. Active group discussion is encouraged over passive slide decks which may, or may not, be read.

PRINCIPLE 15:
CORRELATION IS NOT CAUSATION

A working knowledge of correlation analysis, regression analysis and discriminant analysis is a key part of being able to analyze VoC patterns and look for trends and drivers.

Correlation analysis is a method of statistical evaluation that looks at the strength of the relationship between two continuous variables, X and Y. X could be Customer Satisfaction and Y could be Revenue. If is used to evaluate if one variable tends to trend with another. If they do both trend upwards on their axes, this is known as positive correlation. If they trend in different directions on their axes, this is known as negative correlation. For example, there is a negative correlation between self-esteem and depression' as self-esteem goes up, depression goes down. *Correlation does not, however, tell you that one variable is caused by another.*

Regression analysis is a statistical process that takes a number of predictor variables, X, and interprets with what confidence a change in each will correlate with a change in the dependent variable, Y. If you had a number of potential drivers of customer satisfaction, you would perform regression analysis on them to see which ones are the highest predictors of customer satisfaction.

Discriminant analysis is a statistical analysis that predicts membership in a group or category based on observed values of several continuous variables, X. You may have a number of mutually exclusive categories for soccer player performance during second year tenure at a club such as Highest Performers, Medium Performers and Weakest Performers, along with data of how the athletes performed in their first year. This analysis can, as an example, look at a new team member's stats after their first year and, based on their numbers, predict which category the player will fall into in their second year.

PRINCIPLE 16:
CX DATA SHOULD BE SHARED WITH EVERYONE

As part of fostering organizational adoption of CX practices and customer-centric culture in a business, CX data should be shared with everyone. This helps to create a level of transparency and buy-in from staff across the entire organization.

In the past, data would fall into the hands of a few key decision makers. Today the trend has been towards making sure *relevant* data falls into every employee's hands along with actionable insights they can use to make a difference. This helps empower employees and give them a greater sense of the customer's success and what a great experience means to them.

I use the term *relevant*, because what an employee needs to see in the call center will likely be different than a high level executive, who will likely want an easily digestible dashboard with overall trends and top priorities.

What all of this means is simple: you move from a handful of CX related decisions per year, by a few individuals, to empowering thousands of small decisions, daily, throughout the organization by every employee. Combine this with an effective culture and governance system and the organization will be set up to deliver great customer experiences.

PRINCIPLE 17:
EXPERIMENTS SHOULD TEST THE BIGGEST RISKS

Design Thinking formally introduced a concept to the business world that has been around for some time in the software engineering world: evolutionary prototyping. Prototyping with customers is a great way to build out and test new products and ideas quickly and cheaply, while remaining laser focused on customer needs and receiving instant feedback from them. Just remember to focus on the underlying JTBD, not necessarily the product or idea.

Experiments like this are a low-cost way of filling in details related to key questions that may represent huge risk to an organization.

In Principle 14 we looked at how Kohl's ran an experiment that represented huge risk. Any time you are rolling out something new related to your offerings, targeting new customers or changing the way you operate, you are inviting risk. These are all good cases to use experiments.

When working with customers on iterative design or ideation, it is always a good idea to keep in mind three types of customers.

1) Existing Customers – can tell you what works and what doesn't
2) Customers captured by competitors – can help you understand market segmentation better and underlying JTBD of these groups
3) Customers not consuming in your market – can help you understand growth opportunities that your competitors are not capturing

PRINCIPLE 18:
CX STRATEGY IS A PLAN, NOT A SLOGAN

Many businesses often fail to create succinct and clear business strategies. They often confuse them with basic mission statements, or go too far in the opposite direction and create thick binders that end up sitting on shelves and gathering dust.

A strategy is all about identifying:

- Where you are – your baseline
- Where you want to be
- How to get there

A good CX Strategy should do the following, with the above in mind:

- Specify the target customers
- Specify the branded experience(s) and how customers will think, act and feel when participating in them
- Articulate the unique value proposition and how that will be marketed to set correct expectations
- Outline how the CX strategy will support the business goals
- Specify how the employees will execute the experience so it matches expectations
- Specify which experiences and touchpoints will be prioritized.
- Define metrics to track progress

A communication plan is also vital.

Chuck Martin, former VP at IBM, said: "*The result of bad communication is a disconnection between strategy and execution.*" *Patrick Lencioni* lists *Clarity* as one of the main attributes of Organizational Health in his seminal work,

The Advantage: Why Organizational Health Trumps Everything Else in Business.

SECTION 2

SAMPLE QUESTIONS

QUESTION 1:

Which of the following is the BEST way to gain executive buy-in to a Customer Experience program?

A)   Show examples of other businesses that have improved revenue using CX approaches
B)   Build an alliance of influencers within the organization and have them co-present to the CEO with you
C)   Show how CX metrics can tie to existing business metrics
D)   Explain to the CEO that if the organization does not act quickly, it will miss the CX boat

QUESTION 2:

You have been asked to help a business that is struggling to implement a VoC strategy. The lead CX strategist worked alone and walked out in the middle of the project on bad terms; nobody seems to know where anything stands. After gathering all of their retrievable documentation, what is the next BEST course of action?

A) Inventory known existing surveys and listening posts to try and establish a baseline
B) Analyze data and look for existing VoC data patterns
C) Call the person who left and see if you can pick their brains about where they were in the process
D) Ask frontline staff for help

QUESTION 3:

Which of the following is the BEST way to try to ensure success when implementing a new CX program?

A) Pick the perfect set of Metrics
B) Buy the best analytics software
C) Align the organization
D) Hire the best CX team

QUESTION 4:

When sharing CX data with employees, which of the following is the BEST strategy:

A) Share all CX data whenever it is available
B) Share key data at quarterly meetings
C) Share key data across the organization, with tailored information for each team
D) Share all CX data weekly

QUESTION 5:

Which of the following is the WORST approach to CX improvement:

A) Ensure issues are prevented from re-occurring
B) Adding wow moments to delight customers
C) Fix inconsistent experiences
D) Reducing pain points across key touchpoints

QUESTION 6:

Which of the following is the BEST way to engage employees in CX efforts?

A) Put a CX Strategy Plan on the Intranet for them to read
B) Have Frontline staff share customer stories every week
C) Send weekly communications stressing customer-centricity
D) Implement regular training and coaching across the business

QUESTION 7:

Which of the following is NOT TRUE

A) Every touchpoint can affect a Customer's experience
B) The overall experience is more important than individual touchpoints
C) Touchpoints are typically designed by the organization
D) Only moments of truth can affect a Customer's experience

QUESTION 8:

What is the BEST way to begin building a strong customer centric culture?

A) Hire people with a natural affinity for customers
B) Train staff regularly in customer centricity
C) Share customer stories regularly across the business
D) Build a Customer Room

QUESTION 9:

Which of the following techniques will help place data into mutually exclusive categories as part of VoC insight generation?

A) Regression Analysis
B) Discriminant Analysis
C) Class-based Analysis
D) Correlation Analysis

QUESTION 10:

Which of the following is the best spark to jumpstart VoC efforts?

A) Gathering VoE (Voice of the Employee)
B) Empathy training
C) Inventory of surveys and listening posts
D) Bring in a consulting firm to talk to employees about VoC

QUESTION 11:

Which of the following is the WORST way to prioritize CX improvement projects?

A) Keep a top-ten list of CX Improvement Projects
B) Prioritize by importance to customer and importance to the business
C) Prioritize by Asset Class
D) Prioritize by lowest rated touchpoints

QUESTION 12:

Which of the following is the WORST technique to learn more about why a customer had a bad experience?

A) Ethnographic research
B) Open-ended survey questions
C) One-on-one interviews with the client
D) Analyzing Issue Description in the Ticketing system

QUESTION 13:

Which of the following call center data will BEST help us to understand if re-occurrence of an issue is being prevented?

A) Ticket reopened?
B) Ticket Resolved on first contact?
C) Issue Type
D) Resolution time

QUESTION 14:

Which of the following is always NOT TRUE?

A) The overall experience matters more to customers than individual touchpoints
B) You should understand customer journey stages before touchpoints
C) Only moments of truth change how a customer feels about an experience
D) The higher the perceived value, the more a customer will be willing to pay

QUESTION 15:

After performing a correlation analysis, you notice one variable, X, is trending upwards as the other, Y, trends downward. Which of the following statements is TRUE about this scenario:

A) X going up causes Y to go down
B) X going down causes Y to go up
C) X has a negative correlation with Y
D) X has a positive correlation with Y

QUESTION 16:

Which of the following is MOST LIKELY to cause poorly coordinated execution?

A) Poor communication
B) Poor training
C) Poor culture
D) Poor customer skills

QUESTION 17:

Which of the following is the BEST case for iterative prototyping by the business?

A) A new training course for employees
B) A new performance management system for employees
C) A new product add-on for customers
D) A new pricing structure for customers

QUESTION 18:

Which of the following is the LEAST important skill when leading a CX transformation project:

A) Being able to mobilize others
B) Translating customer metrics into company KPIs for executives
C) GANTT chart skills
D) Storytelling skills

QUESTION 19:

Which of the following is NOT an attribute of Design Thinking?

A) Divergent thinking
B) Use of metaphor
C) Use of prototyping
D) Brand thinking

QUESTION 20:

All of the following are key elements of a Customer Journey Map, EXCEPT:

A) Customer Persona
B) Customer Steps
C) Emotion Graph
D) Timeline

QUESTION 21:

All of the following are key elements of a Customer Persona, EXCEPT:

A) Expectations
B) Years in position
C) Key pain points
D) Most important tasks

QUESTION 22:

Which of the following is NOT a type of CX metric?

A) Prescriptive
B) Descriptive
C) Outcome
D) Perception

QUESTION 23:

All of the following are highly likely to involve exposure to new risk, EXCEPT:

A) Expanding operational processes
B) Expanding offerings to new customer segments
C) Expanding products to new markets
D) Expanding sales to reach more customers in existing segments

QUESTION 24:

Which of the following is NOT a likely benefit of closing the loop with customers:

A) Likely increase in Share of Wallet
B) Likely increase in customers providing feedback in future
C) Likely increase in customers who will recommend business
D) Likely increase in future survey response rates

QUESTION 25:

Which of the following is a metric used to capture the percentage of customers with the most positive opinions of your business?

A) Top Box
B) Net Promoter
C) Customer Satisfaction Index
D) Perception

QUESTION 26:

Closing the loop lets your customers know all of the following, EXCEPT:

A) Their feedback has been received
B) You value their input
C) Their feedback is going to be used to make improvements
D) You will make the changes they have requested

QUESTION 27:

Which of the following can be used to perform Root Cause Analysis?

A) Ishikawa Diagram
B) Pareto Chart
C) A/B Testing
D) Scatter Diagrams

QUESTION 28:

Which of the following can be used to prioritize issues?

A) Ishikawa Diagram
B) Pareto Chart
C) A/B Testing
D) Scatter Diagrams

QUESTION 29:

Which of the following is the FIRST thing you should do to begin to align silos?

A) Ask the CEO to talk to each business unit leader
B) Meet individually with silo leaders to gain trust and build credibility
C) Hire a high performing CX team
D) Create a cross-functional CX team with members in each business unit

QUESTION 30:

A customer makes a to-go order but has to wait in-line for a long time to pick up their food, which irritates them. Which one of the following metrics will BEST capture that this pain point exists?

A) Ease of placing order
B) Customer Effort score
C) Quality of food
D) Bottom Box

QUESTION 31:

A piece of software purchased for $60,000 generates additional growth revenue of $90,000 over a three year period. What has been its Return on Investment (ROI)?

A) $30,000
B) $90,000
C) 50%
D) 150%

QUESTION 32:

What is the correct measure to find the most common response to a survey on a scale of 1 to 5?

A. The Mode
B. The Median
C. The Average
D. The Mean

QUESTION 33:

Which of the following methods allows a business to understand customer preference by having them compare various features against one another?

A) Conjoint analysis
B) Regression analysis
C) Preferential analysis
D) Quantitative analysis

QUESTION 34:

A Customer Experience Team is responsible for all of the following, EXCEPT:

A. Nurturing a single company voice across silos
B. Managing call center restructuring
C. Supporting a CX governance system
D. Supporting functional teams with CX training

QUESTION 35:

What is the BEST way to ensure Customers perceive value during their customer experience?

A. By aligning operational touchpoints with the brand promise
B. By setting low expectations
C. By performing detailed analysis of customer Jobs-to-be-done
D. By shifting funds to execution and letting word-of-mouth dictate marketing

QUESTION 36:

Which of the following is the BEST way to motivate employees to focus on the customer?

A. Tell a customer success story at the beginning of every meeting
B. Set up bonuses for all call center staff tied to ticket resolution time
C. Set up bonuses for all staff tied to overall customer satisfaction
D. Create a Customer Room

QUESTION 37:

What is the BEST method to understand the root cause of why a customer hung up on a staff member and then provided a score of '1' on their NPS survey?

A. Call the customer and ask why
B. Check the history for first contact resolutions for this customer
C. Check the call holding time for this ticket
D. Analyze all operational data for this ticket

QUESTION 38:

A new cinema chain is about to open. Which of the following BEST describes who their competitors are?

A. Other cinema chains in the town
B. Other cinema chains within an hour's drive
C. Other cinema chains within an hour's drive, plus on-demand video and DVD stores
D. Any business able to provide entertainment to the customer

QUESTION 39:

Which of the following BEST describes a business that has many VoC listening posts and employees who do everything they can for customers, but does not have a process in place to follow through with CX improvements?

A) Strong culture, strong governance
B) Strong culture, weak governance
C) Weak culture, weak governance
D) Weak culture, strong governance

QUESTION 40:

You are invited to speak to local business owners about Customer Experience. A CEO asks why businesses should care about this domain. Which of the following is the BEST answer?

A) Customer Experience is about doing the right thing
B) Modern business is no longer just about profit
C) Customer Experience provides a path to a competitive advantage
D) Modern business competes exclusively on customer satisfaction

SECTION 3

ANSWERS & EXPLANATIONS

QUESTION 1:

Principle 9 teaches us that everything in the world of CX comes back to the bottom line. An executive leadership team is more likely to back a CX program if they are confident that it will pay dividends.

Thus options **B** and **D** are not correct. This leaves us with a choice between **A** and **C**. Whilst A could be very useful, **C** is a much more exact approach where a clear link can be made between CX metrics and business metrics.

C is the correct answer.

QUESTION 2:

In order to implement a strategy of any kind you first must know where you are starting from, so you know what needs to be improved. The question states that nobody seems to know where the CX work stands. Thus **A** is the correct answer as you will need to take stock of the work conducted so far as part of a larger effort to baseline where the organization currently stands from a CX perspective. **See Principle 18**.

A is the correct answer.

QUESTION 3:

The best way to ensure a successful CX implementation is to make sure that the organization is coordinated and aligned. See **Principle 10**. **A, B** and **D** are all tactical solutions that may work in individual silos but not necessarily across the business.

C is the correct answer.

QUESTION 4:

When sharing CX information within an organization, we should remember **Principle 16**. Relevant information should be shared with everyone. **B** and **D** focus on very specific times which will cause information gaps. **A** is a good answer but will cause irrelevant information to also be shared.

C is the correct answer.

QUESTION 5:

When looking to improve customer experiences, **Principle 7** teaches us that reliability always trumps 'wow' moments or attempts to 'delight' the customer. Negative experiences are more likely to hurt you than positive experiences are to help you. With that in mind, **A**, **C** and **D** all do a good job of making experiences more reliable, consistent and less painful.

B is the correct answer.

QUESTION 6:

The best way to engage employees in CX efforts is to engage their hearts and minds. People are far more engaged with actions than words; see **Principle 14**. **A** is too passive. **C** is just words in an e-mail, which may or may not be read. And **B** will be great for front line staff, but will have no impact across the rest of the organization.

D is the correct answer.

QUESTION 7:

We know that at every moment a customer interacts with a business, there is a possibility for the customer's experience to be affected. So we know **A** is true. Research has shown that the overall experience is more important to the consumer than individual touchpoints. So we know **B** is also true. And touchpoints are typically designed by the business as they are operational in nature. So **C** is also true. However Moments of Truth, as defined in **Principle 6,** whilst being the most important touchpoints, are not the only ones that can affect a customer's experience.

D is the correct answer.

QUESTION 8:

Culture is what you do when your boss is not in the room! You can provide all of the training possible (**B**), share stories across the business (**C**) and even implement a Customer Room (**D**). But if you don't hire the right people who genuinely care about customers and have natural listening and empathy skills, you are going to find it an uphill battle. The best way to build a strong customer-centric culture is to hire the right people who can then be nurtured with little effort. See **Principle 11**.

A is the correct answer.

QUESTION 9:

Discriminant analysis is used to place data into mutually exclusive categories. See **Principle 15** for a refresher on the types of analysis and their intended use.

B is the correct answer.

QUESTION 10:

Principle 6 teaches us that it is possible to jump-start a VoC effort by using VoE. The voice of the employee is often coupled with VoC efforts but if no VoC data is available, VoE will provide some very useful information to jump-start the initiative. **B** will help staff learn to be more empathetic. **C** will provide a good list of what CX outreach currently exists. And **D** will also be very educational for staff. However none of these can start generating insights.

A is the correct answer.

QUESTION 11:

This question is all about prioritization and trying to find the WORST way of approaching prioritizing CX Improvement initiatives.

In general, **A** is considered a best practice and should be constantly updated. **B** is considered the de facto way to prioritize, using a prioritization matrix and may actually lead to populating the list in option A. **C** is also an established method of prioritizing CX improvement projects based on the customer value.

Principle 5 teaches us to be wary of using touchpoints alone in prioritization. This is due to their operational nature and temptation to focus on the business perspective more than the customer.

D is the correct answer.

QUESTION 12:

The key to this question is WHY. WHY did the customer have a bad experience? **A** and **C** are likely to be the best techniques to solicit the WHY. This is because actions are more reliable than words (**Principle 14**). Being able to observe the client or interact with them one-on-one will most certainly yield a lot of useful, qualitative data. **D** is limited to a description field in a ticketing system, whereas **B** is open-ended and will contain a lot more detailed information.

D is the correct answer.

QUESTION 13:

The key to this question is using the data fields to UNDERSTAND if an issue has re-occurred. **A** tells us if the resolution was UNSUCCESFUL first time around. **B** tells us if the customer service rep was able to RESOLVE the issue on their first attempt. **D** tells us HOW LONG it took to resolve the ticket. None of these can help us understand if the issue is re-occurring.

The Issue Type, however, does. If we see the issue popping up on ticketing data over time, then we know the issue has not truly been fixed. If we never see that issue appear again, we know it was likely prevented from occurring. Prevention is stressed in **Principle 8**.

C is the correct answer.

QUESTION 14:

This question is looking for which answer is always not true. By process of simple elimination, we know that **A** is true. **B** is also true, as illustrated in **Principle 4**. And **Principle 3** teaches us about value and why **D** is also true. As already discussed in question 7, Moments of Truth are not the only touchpoints that can change how a customer feels about an experience.

C is the correct answer.

QUESTION 15:

A and **B** can be immediately ruled out as we know correlation is not causation (**Principle 15**). Therefore the correct answer is either **C** or **D**. And we know that when one value moves up as one moves down (i.e. they move in different directions) this is known as Negative Correlation.

C is the correct answer.

QUESTION 16:

They key to this question is the word 'coordinated.'

Coordination is likely to be affected by communication more than any of the other items. Refer to the quote by Chuck Martin at the end of **Principle 18**.

A is the correct answer.

QUESTION 17:

Iterative Prototyping is something that happens between businesses and customers to rapidly create a solution (**Principle 17**). Therefore options **A** and **B** can be discarded.

Rapidly changing pricing structures with a client (**D**) is not likely to make a good impression and will lower their confidence in the business.

C is the correct answer.

QUESTION 18:

This questions tests your knowledge of Leadership functions Vs Management.

Leading a CX transformation means being able to influence others to join or support your cause. Whilst being able to project manage using GANTT charts is a good skill, it is low down on the list of what is required from a great leader and falls more into management.

A is clearly an influencing skill.

B, whilst a little more technical, is involved with influencing leadership.

D is a classic influencing technique to build empathy.

C is the correct answer.

QUESTION 19:

All of the items listed in this question are facets of Design Thinking, except for **D**.

D is the correct answer.

QUESTION 20:

Customer Persona (**A**), Customer Steps (**B**) and the Timeline (**D**) are all parts of a Customer Journey Map. An emotion graph is not.

C is the correct answer.

QUESTION 21:

Principle 2 shows us that Personas should emphasize expectations (**A**), and list key pain points (**C**) as well as the most important tasks they are trying to complete (jobs to be done) (**D**).

B is the correct answer.

QUESTION 22:

Descriptive (**B**), Outcome (**C**) and Perception (**D**) are all types of CX metrics. For more information see Kerry Bodine's book: _Outside In_.

A is the correct answer.

QUESTION 23:

Any time you increase or change the way you operate (**A**), expand your customer segments (**B**) or increase your product offerings (**C**) you are highly likely to become exposed to new risk. Increasing sales to a customer segment you are already familiar with (**D**) is not likely to add any new risks.

D is the correct answer.

QUESTION 24:

In her excellent 2012 article, _"Tips to Help You Close the Loop with Your Customers"_, Annette Franz talks extensively about the benefits of closing the loop with customers.
http://www.cx-journey.com/2012/04/tips-to-help-you-close-loop-with-your.html

In her article, she lists **B**, **C** and **D** as likely benefits of closing the loop. However, you are unlikely to increase share of wallet (**A**) until you _act_ on the feedback (**Principle 14**) and improve the customer experience and perceived value (**Principle 3**).

A is the correct answer.

QUESTION 25:

Top Box (**A**) is the only option that looks specifically at the % of responses that gave the highest possible rating.

A is the correct answer.

QUESTION 26:

Closing the loop with customers is a way to let customers know that their feedback has been received (**A**), that you value their feedback (**B**) and that their feedback will be used to make improvements (**C**). What it does not guarantee is that their suggestions and requests will be implemented.

D is the correct answer.

QUESTION 27:

Pareto Charts (**B**) are typically used to help prioritize work. A/B Testing (**C**) is a testing technique to compare two versions of a web site. Scatter Diagrams (**D**) are used to plot two variables on a graph, typically to test correlation. Ishikawa diagrams (**A**), also known as *fishbone diagrams*, are used to help structure thinking in root cause analysis.

A is the correct answer.

QUESTION 28:

Pareto Charts (**B**) are typically used to help prioritize work. They are often associated with the 80/20 rule that shows roughly 80% of issues are caused by 20% of the defects, thus helping illuminate the key 20% of work that should be prioritized.

B is the correct answer.

QUESTION 29:

Principle 10 teaches that the best way to align the silos is to treat the work like a political campaign and meet with leaders across the organization to gain trust and build credibility (**B**). Asking the CEO to step in (**A**) will not help to empower you. Hiring or creating a CX team (**C** and **D**) won't do much in the way of influencing leaders and team members of each silo.

B is the correct answer.

QUESTION 30:

Measuring the ease of placing the order (**A**) will not help identify the irritating wait which follows placing the order. The same is true for the quality of the food (**C**) which is also unrelated. Bottom Box (**D**) is only concerned with the % of customers who gave the lowest rating. Customer Effort (**B**) measures the amount of effort or hassle a customer has in realizing their job-to-be-done. If they become irritated by the wait, the number on the Customer Effort score will be sufficient to flag there is an issue for follow up.

B is the correct answer.

QUESTION 31:

The most basic formula to calculate ROI is:

(Growth - Cost) / Cost = ROI

Therefore this would translate to:

(90,000-60,000) / 60,000

= 30,000 / 60,000

= 0.5 or 50%

Remember ROI is always expressed as a percentage.

C is the correct answer.

QUESTION 32:

The Mean (**D**) and The Average (**C**) are the same number, which is produced by adding up every response and dividing by the number of responses. The Median (**B**) is the number occurring at exactly the middle of all responses; if there were 11 responses ranked in order (e.g. 1,1,1,1,1,2,2,3,3,4,5) it would be the 6th number (in this case: 2). The Mode (**A**) is the response that occurs with most frequency; in this case: 1.

A is the correct answer.

QUESTION 33:

The technique that allows a business to understand customer preference by having them compare various features against one another is known as conjoint analysis (**A**). **B** is a statistical technique that involves no customer interaction. **C** is made up. **D** is just a broad umbrella term for many different types of numeric techniques.

A is the correct answer.

QUESTION 34:

The role of the CX team is to integrate and support organizational adoption of CX ownership and best practices across the business. With this in mind, it is very easy to deduce which answer does not relate to CX best practices – **B**.

Answer **A** is embodied in **Principle 10**. Answer **C** is embodied in **Principle 12**. Answer **D** is mentioned as part of **Principle 11**.

B is the correct answer.

QUESTION 35:

The best way to ensure customers perceive value during their customer experience is to ensure their expectations match exactly the delivered experience. This is the essence of **Principle 3**.

Setting low expectations (**B**) is not a winning game plan for any business. Performing detailed analysis of customer JTBD (**C**) is all well and good, but tells us nothing about the follow through and how that may be communicated in the brand promise. Focusing on execution while abandoning marketing (**D**) completely gives up any control the business may have over setting expectations.

A is the correct answer.

QUESTION 36:

As we learned in **Principle 11**, bonuses (**B** and **C**) are not the best way to motivate employees to focus on the customer, and can many times have a negative effect on the customer experience. Creating a Customer Room (**D**) is a good idea, but will be worthless unless employees actively engage with it. Storytelling (**A**) is a fantastic way to bring the realities of the customer into employee's hearts and minds.

A is the correct answer.

QUESTION 37:

Principle 13 teaches us that big data cannot tell you WHY. And that is the key word in this question. First Contact resolutions (**B**), Holding time (**C**) and all operational data (**D**) are quantitative in nature. Of the options listed, simply picking up the phone and calling the customer (**A**) is actually the best way to get to the WHY.

A is the correct answer.

QUESTION 38:

This question is concerned with framing a market. **Principle 1** teaches that markets should be framed in terms of Jobs to be done. In terms of finding the BEST answer, whichever option provides the broadest estimate while still remaining accurate will be the best.

Thinking in terms of set theory, **A** is a sub-set of B. **B** is a sub-set of C. **C** is a sub-set of D. And **D** is still accurate.

Whilst providing entertainment might be the best answer, there might still be better answers if the cinema chain does more than simply provide entertainment. If it meets other jobs to be done, businesses also satisfying those JTBD should be considered competitors as well.

D is the correct answer.

QUESTION 39:

The business has employees who do everything they can for their customers, which indicates a very strong customer centric culture. This helps us deduce the correct answer to one of two options – **A** and **B**. However if the necessary governance structures to help with follow through have not been created, the business will falter in its CX execution. **Principle 12** reminds us that culture + governance = execution.

B is the correct answer.

QUESTION 40:

As illuminated in **Principle 9**, the end goal of adopting a strong CX strategy is to increase value, which ultimately yields an improved bottom line. The CEO's job is to ensure their business is providing a good ROI to its shareholders and/or owners.

It is incorrect to say that modern business exclusively competes on customer satisfaction (**D**). Customer satisfaction will likely be one of the metrics a business uses to compete but not the only one. Saying Customer Experience is about doing the right thing (**A**) might sound nice and fluffy but it is not going to be taken seriously as a reason to adopt CX practices by any CEO.

Saying that modern business is no longer just about profit (**B**), whilst a statement that many would agree with, is still not a compelling reason to adopt CX practices, as it says nothing specifically about them. The reason needs to resonate with CEOs and convince them that the effort is going to be good for their business in the long run. And studies show that Customer Experience does provide a competitive advantage.

C is the correct answer.

SECTION 4

ARE YOU CCXP READY?

PRACTICE MAKES PERFECT

Once you have used this book and feel that you might be ready to take the exam, I would strongly recommend taking a practice exam or two. Practice exams can be very helpful as they allow you to experience the exam conditions and allow your mind and body to become more resilient to the testing experience. In fact they can end up making the difference between passing and failing.

I remember when I took my first CCXP exam – I did some breathing exercises and had myself in a very calm, zen-like state. Then I hit the BEGIN EXAM button and the first question appeared along with the timer counting down. My heart rate soared and I was flushed with adrenaline! This disorienting experience can cause you to misread questions and over-think answers. I honestly did not feel prepared. However, the second time around I was ready; mainly as I knew what to expect.

In September and October 2017, knowing that the CCXP exam was going to be changing, I locked myself away in my office and, through hours upon hours of research, was able to divide up the six core CCXP competencies into 36 individual knowledge areas. I then began writing practice questions at different levels for each. I ended up creating a CCXP Exam Simulator unlike anything on the market and which I believe to be completely future proof against newer versions of the exam: **CCXPExamSimulator.com**

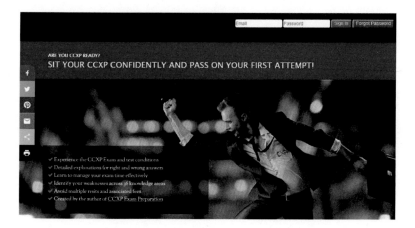

The simulator mimics the exam conditions, so you will be presented with questions of equal or greater difficulty.

After each exam, you can go back and step through your answers to see where you went off track. The EXPERT package will even generate a personalized study plan for you to close any knowledge gaps identified. Below is a partial screen shot showing what the 'review' mode looks like.

Question 1:
Which of the following statements is NOT TRUE regarding front line staff training?

A:	Creating clean, measurable operational targets will help employees focus on providing a great customer experience. ✓
B:	Providing soft skills training will be more useful in the long run than a cheat-sheet of how to solve the top 10 most common issues raised by customers. ✗
C:	Training should start at employee on-boarding and become an ongoing activity.
D:	Training provided by experienced training providers will, in general, be more helpful than training provided by a direct Supervisor.

Explanation:
Simply creating a target does not guarantee a great customer experience or employee focus. Without execution to back it up, a target is nothing more than wishful thinking.

The simulator was launched January 2018.

At the end of the year I am going to be taking all of the taxable profits from the sales and awarding them to a number of animal shelters and rescues. These people work endless hours trying to keep dogs and cats alive – many animals wind up in kill shelters and the rescue community has to scramble at the 11th hour to get them moved into safe rescues.

My mission is to help people do right by animals by helping businesses do right by their customers. If you know of a rescue who you would like to nominate for some of these funds, please drop me a line at **Mike@MeasureOfTruth.co**

APPENDIX A

MORE INFO ON CHARITIES

TRI-LAKES HUMANE SOCIETY

Web: http://www.tri-lakeshumanesoc.org/
Facebook: https://www.facebook.com/TriLakesHS/
Paypal: pets4u@centurylink.net
Mailing address for checks: PO BOX 588, Reeds Spring, MO 65737

BASSET AND BEAGLE RESCUE OF THE HEARTLAND

Web: http://bassetandbeagle.org/
Facebook: https://www.facebook.com/BassetAndBeagle/
Paypal: donate@bassetandbeagle.org
Mailing address for checks: PO Box 554, Boys Town, NE 68010

PAWS AND HANDS UNITED

Web: http://www.pawsandhandsunited.org/
Facebook: https://www.facebook.com/PawsandHandsUnited/
Paypal: info@pawsandhandsunited.com
Mailing address for checks: 261 Dawn Road, Branson, MO 65616

TRIANGLE BEAGLE RESCUE

Web: http://www.tribeagles.org/
Facebook: https://www.facebook.com/tribeagles/
Paypal: give@tribeagles.org
Mailing address for checks: 2664 Timber Dr. Suite 344, Garner, NC 27529

HUMANE SOCIETY OF SOUTHWEST MISSOURI

Web: http://www.swh.org/
Facebook: https://www.facebook.com/humanesocietyofsouthwestmissouri/
Paypal: sbolding@hsswmo.org
Mailing address for checks: 3161 W. Norton Road, Springfield, Missouri 65803

Made in the USA
Lexington, KY
01 August 2018

PRINCIPLE 5:
ALWAYS PRIORITIZE

Once you have your broad phases of your customer journeys, you can begin breaking them down into touchpoints. These then need to be prioritized. There are numerous ways of doing this. You can use a simple **Prioritization Matrix** with *Importance to Customer* on one axis and *importance to Business* on the other. You can also use **Conjoint Analysis, Regression Analysis, Pareto charts** or **Asset Classes** to prioritize. These are also relevant when you come to prioritize journeys and even customers. You can't improve everything, so this has to happen. One way to help with prioritization is to create a top ten list of improvement projects.

Proceed with this word of caution, however: touchpoints are always operational since they are designed by the business. By focusing too heavily on touchpoints, it is easy to slip into looking at the operational aspects of the company and not what the customer is thinking, doing and feeling.

Operational aspects are, however, important when considering the interdependencies across people, process and technology that impact delivery of the customer experience. For example, CX data may show that there is frustration at being put on hold for long periods of time by call center staff. Further deep dives into the operational aspects may show that the call center staff are reaching out to other teams for help and not receiving timely responses.

These insights will lead into a list of improvement opportunities. And these will – you guessed it – need to be prioritized!